POEMS, PLAIN AND APPLIED

POEMS, PLAIN AND APPLIED

DENNIS R. KEEFE

Illustrated by

LOUISA KEEFE

Copyright © 2009 by Dennis R. Keefe.

ISBN: Softcover   978-1-4415-9557-7

All rights reserved. No part of this book may be reproduced or transmitted in any form or by any means, electronic or mechanical, including photocopying, recording, or by any information storage and retrieval system, without permission in writing from the copyright owner.

This book was printed in the United States of America.

To order additional copies of this book, contact:
Xlibris Corporation
1-888-795-4274
www.Xlibris.com
Orders@Xlibris.com

Table of Contents

From Here

1. How's Your Day? 11
2. Bed Rappings 13
3. What Is Temporary? 15
4. Aging's Gray Areas 16
5. Senior, Rise 18
6. A Poet Takes the Day Off 20

With the Family

1. On Track 23
2. Cycle-logical 24
3. Table Talk 26
4. Thanks to Olivia 28
5. Hannah's Banana Boat 31
6. Emily Goes to School 32
7. A Litany to Alyssa 33
8. Girlwind 37
9. Baby Roomba 38
10. Fathers' Days—Do Count 39
11. Molly in the Garden 41
12. The Kitchen Truck 42
13. Uncovering the Magic 44
14. Around the Playground 47
15. Edges 49

And the Help of Some Friends

1. Getting Somewhere 55
2. Among the Young 56

3. Look at Me 57
4. A Couple of Toos 58
5. Gentleman Jag 59
6. Junior-Senior Prom 60
7. Lauds 63
8. Who's Your Lazarus? 65
9. Ghosts in the Quad 66
10. Your Place or Mine? 68
11. Beauty Pallor 69
12. Car Wars 70

We Experience our Backyard

1. Dinner With Theater on the Lawn 75
2. The Last Bird Words 77
3. Backyard Summer Drama 78
4. November Between 81
5. The Hawk Feeder 82
6. Backyard Hummer 83

Other Special Places

1. A Beach Night Plug 87
2. Hiking Yellowstone 88
3. Huron Shoreline 91
4. Dead End 92
5. The Point of the Mission 93
6. Lighting a Mall Pall 95
7. Fire in the Peat 96
8. A Rube Cubed 98
9. Chaos in the House 101
10. Sign Irony 103
11. A Vineyard Picnic Space 105
12. Maybe Next Year 106
13. Ain't We Got fun 108
14. Holiday Travels 111
15. The News From the Cruise 113

And Some Amazing Events

1. An M & M Wedding Toast 129
2. Nouveau 133
3. Travels to the Sun 138
4. Olivia Turns Seven 142
5. Are You Being Served?... 143
6. Give Me a Break 144
7. Movers and Shapers 147
8. A Pillar Raised 151
9. Two Queens... 153
10. Lighting Veterans' Day 157

From Here

How's Your Day Going?

Are you asking me,
biased and moody though I be?
A more objective echo
might better reflect and rate the data
steaming in today. Check them out.
Give a listen. Let's get your opinion.

The floor was solid,
meeting me this morning
as I left my bed,
the first event of my day of—
yes—few surprises.
Last night's rain stayed outside.
The machines timed their washing,
let me shower
and the water tempressure stabilize
—minimal fiddling.

The needed people showed up today.
My wife emerged to share coffee and newspaper.
A call from our son meant
his kids went
to school today—
grandparent interventions not required.

That coffee I made was . . . right on.
The paper arrived in its box on
time and the walk to the street to get it,
springtime fine.

No irritating fools on the road,
though no one was interviewed but me.

Wish I could be as upbeat about my body.
It moved, grudgingly,
its usual aches and pains
about average for guys like me—
At least, no new rebellions yet today.
I know. Not exactly world peace.
I'll take another shot at that tomorrow.

And I don't expect to meet
any heathens needing conversion on the street.
I thought up an excuse to skip
our church's mission trip
meeting this week.

If things continue on this way—
I will do okay
but wonder—

from over yonder—

how you see my day.
It's almost noon.
How am I doin'?

Bed Rappings

      There is a comforter in my bed
        but troubles in my head.
      Is there a 911 I can call?

Wrapped in warmth I
    feel my covers say
        stay,
but 'neath my hair
    nightmares prowl
    ear to ear
        keeping sleep at bay.

In that private parade there may
    be
threatened children
a coveted wife
waters dark
fires from a spark
or a man with a knife.

To make matters worse
    I begin rhyming verse.
Should I leave my bed
    write a verse instead
or will that make
    getting up a curse?

Into the comforter
    sinking deep
my wife falls
    further into sleep.

I could dissolve all this
    and straighten my head—
lean over,

      kiss—
trade a messed up sleep
for a mussed up bed
      wrappings and all.
Or . . .
      I could keep her out
          of this abyss
and wait for the healing sun to call.

Most likely,
      once again,
the parade will start.
      And the fires with the sparks . . .

What Is Temporary?

I don't usually choose
to park this close—
unlike those
who sport
handicapper signs.
Parking lots
help me exercise.

And this cane
you think you see
is actually
a mountain hiking stick.

I say I'm practicing.
In reality
it steadies my walk
and helps me manage
my sciatica.

The stick, it"s just temporary.
Freedom will come with surgery.

But it is normal for
old spines to collapse.
So I may keep my stick—
stow it there
with all my other
hiking gear.

Aging's Gray Areas

Devoid of angst, I
ponder my senior high,
and note the exchange—
gnarly knees and slipping memory
for . . . a few organs yet to fail
plus . . . this comforting loss of anxiety,
      that old companion that tagged along
      and ragged so long on me.

But, mind,
there are issues hear
that should be discussed.
You (geezers) in the chair(s),
come stroll.
We'll air
our thoughts, explore
some of the highs and lows
of growing old.

Would you agree,
people move at a disturbing rate today?
I think it's the expanding universe.
It creates longer distances everywhere.
They have to hurry to compensate.

I prefer to walk with care,
the better to see what is
out there.
So, as we stroll
can we take a deliberate pace?

What's that? Can't hear?
Too far way?
Yes, you and I could teach today
a thing or two.
We never had trouble speaking clear.

Not too fast; let's catch a breath.
I meant to ask
about your . . . nose . . . ,
yes, aromas.
Can you make sense
of the scents of the world?
Our senior years, are they to be
more delicate, aromatically?

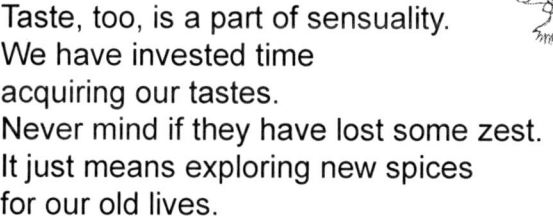

Taste, too, is a part of sensuality.
We have invested time
acquiring our tastes.
Never mind if they have lost some zest.
It just means exploring new spices
for our old lives.

And touch—
You have, no doubt, been told
—to avoid getting old—
"Don't lose touch with your environment."
Well, . . . , do you sense this chill in the air?
We could step inside. It's warmer there.

But before we do, accept my thanks.
Your company has helped me work things through.

True, it takes some courage to survive.
But there are assets which accrue
to those past sixty-five.

We just need to utilize . . .
Maybe tomorrow, after rise and shine.

In the meantime, from inside here, looking out
things seem much
the same.

Senior, Rise

Have you met your organs lately?
Have they come knocking on the door
with new found complaints
about quality of work-life at the store?
With luck there are some that haven't failed as yet,
maybe one or two.

If the news from the scales is not so good,
a new life style might be due.
Weight Watchers and a thyroid boost helped me.
But, I seem to recall a Mark Twain thing,
"What helped me may assassinate you,"
You sort it through.

That heart you never noticed,
does it shimmy, shake or flutter?
How many procedures have you tried?
And did they make things any better?

How about your lower back,
your upper neck,
those disks they haven't fused as yet?

Sound like you?
You may becoming senior-ized.

I'm not just talking senior eyes

but ears, memory and a whole lot more,
things that will no longer be ignored—
an organ concerto, if you will,
of instruments in dissonance
which know
to penetrate your hearing now
they have to screech and yell.

If this is you, senior, rise.
You've projects to complete.
You've heard the advice
about getting up and moving on.

Did you remember to write it down?

A Poet Takes the Day Off

Gone today:
Bird watching sessions,
leisurely conversations
with the back porch muse
and critter news.

Inspiration Point, special events,
can you hold your effects,
issue rain checks?
I travel today with more intent,
unrelaxed—
less wander, less wonder.

I have given my eyes and ears,
my nose for the noise of words
the morning off.

Sent to recharge and
return refreshed,
they disappeared
without committing a time to me—
reserving, I surmise,
their usual element of surprise.

So here I am
with unpoetic urgency—
and uncharacteristic zip.
The change refreshes,
this mission trip.
Let them watch me for a change,
conjure their own verses.
My wife's car needs oil
and the appointment is
at ten.

With the Family

On Track

I meet her occasionally;
we touch, talk,
remain briefly side by side.
Then, unique in stride,
we separate,
a step at a time—
she, jogging, doing,
not pressing me;
I, walking, composing,
not slowing her.

Amazing grace and gravity
maintain the orbit
circling our commonality.

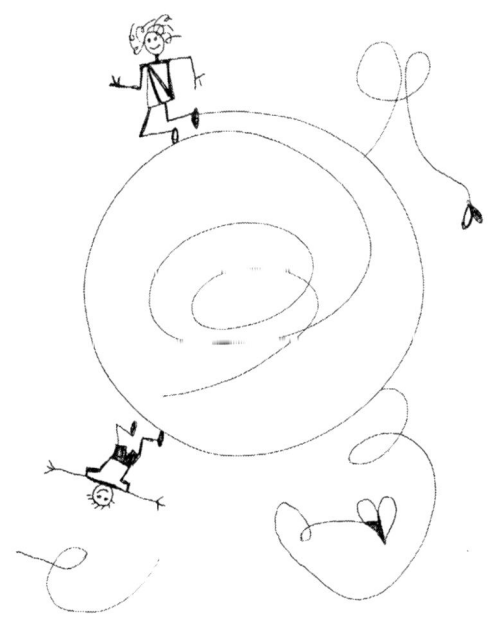

Cycle-logical—
Press For Go

From many rooms, one
laundry grouped and basket batched.
Here's the rest.

From one, many
sorts:
shirts and shorts
colors, whites
frillies, heavies,
wash and wear.
Wash the worn.
Reach for bleach or
hope in soap.
Batten down and button down.

If wash, then dry.
Wash AND dry (not or);
dry or not wash.
Some we skip and drip
but more oftener we add the softener.
Stuff the dryer;
Twist and click.

Unstuff
and basket batch.
Then sort and match.
Fold OR (not and) hang.
Those requiring ironing,
Press then dress;
If dress, first press
press or no dress

From one to many.
Distribute
rooms, closets, drawers
choosers and users,
and, lo,
Return to go.

Table Talk

Everyone's here,
table seated,
let's begin with a prayer
and eat what's heated.
But, pray, tonight,
can we share more than food?
An event from the day to relate?
An interlude
from the routine,
set the scene,
create a mood?

I ate
for lunch
super-sized fries
and apple pies
with a Nestle Crunch.

No, no.
something important
not about food.

It would be important to me
if you would pass
the peas, potato salad and pimento cheese.

How about russets?
They're bakers,
the best.

No, not potato talk,
table talk.
You know, chew the fat.
Damn!
Why did I say that?

Now that you mention it,
the meat is tough.
But, hey!
"Good for your jaw muscles,"
parents would say.
When food and times were rough
we ate what was there.
Now that there's plenty,
We pretend to be picky
but eat anything
anywhere.

Enough! Enough!
This isn't a trough!
This focus on food is fraught
with naught.
No thoughts to talk?
Dinner's done.
I quit; you've won.
If you can't leave and run,
just walk.

Of course, but first
is there dessert?

Thanks to Olivia

Olivia came to live with us
and she brought her mommy too
Now we have pretty furniture,
new rugs and a piano—who
do you think is learning
"Doe, a deer, a female deer . . . ?"

Olivia came to live with us
and now we're learning to share
our dog and minivan
but we don't care;
she brought more grandparents
an aunt and uncles.
Fair is fair.

Olivia came to live with us
and now we can't sit still
we've traded cable for
tennis, swimming,
dance and yoga
     to name a few.
They say it's all to have some fun
but it makes us sleepy too.

Olivia came to live with us
and helped us shape our ship
we've planted a garden
trimmed the yard
and generally fixed things up.
We even took a trip
to Disney World
and did it up
real proud.

Olivia came to live with us
now there's music everywhere
for Livi's mom sings, plays and teaches at the U.
She taught us handbells and
'Tho we struggle to reach the keys and pedals
we're learning piano too.

Olivia came to live with us
I guess our daddy liked her some
because he married her mom.

Hannah's Banana Boat

A Birthday Boat for Hannah
approaching age 4

They stopped for lunch
at The Banana Boat
next door to some boaters
near the Florida shore.
Now Hannah
has a banana
boat in mind for when she turns four.

In Hannah's mind it's not a toy.
It's real;
It's big . . .
" . . . big enough for all of us to ride on."

Hannah's boat is a source of joy,
shaped like a banana,
topped with a flag and a triangle sail.
A rainbow concoction that
"needs to have all the colors in it."

Hannah wonders through her three-year-old eyes,
able to see beyond boat rides:
"How would we take it out of the water?
And how would we take it home?"

With a few more Hannahs to bring us together,
to cram us, crowd us, gather us in boats,
bringing along every color and sailor—
wouldn't that be a ride?
And when done with sailing fun,
we'd build that banana boat's trailer.

Emily Goes to School

Emily's family has a new focus this year
For Emmy's first school day is finally here.
Preschool is done
Kindergarten roundup was fun.
Now play days are school days,
just beginning the run
through teachers and friends,
classes and grades,
year after year.
Will it ever be done?

They will help her get better
at this and at that
learning numbers, letters
and how to spell "CAT."

Ideas will be taught
how to march through her mind
in formations of phrases,
new words and new books;
adding, subtracting and art—
maybe she'll even learn how to cook,
as she discovers the gold mine
that is hers for a lifetime
one that will deepen, grow bigger—
similar, but different
from yours and from mine.

Thanks, mom and dad,
for getting her there;
the time will go fast,
and you will be proud;
just remember your role in the cast:
you can't cheer too loud.

A Litany to Alyssa

on the Transition to Three

At last it's time
We can all breathe free
Thanks be to God,
Alyssa's turned three.

They say she was a "terrible two."
Thanks be to God,
I suppose she's just really
like me and like you.

Alyssa was determined to
have her own way.
Now that she's three
will she need less attention?
"Stop, look and listen to me."
Thanks be to God
for now she turns three.

ON THIS TRIP, WHO WILL TAKE ALYSSA WITH THEM?

When she had our attention what did she do?
(How many things can a two-year-old do?)
With two sisters to teach her
just watch her:

throwing toys
smearing chocolate
hitting boys,
girls, dogs and adults
spilling drinks
talking blue streaks

dripping bottles on the floor
emptying trash cans and table drawers
Harassing Kaylee,
Demanding candy
And climbing a tree—

Two hands, better than one;
Putting Papa on the run
when hanging and screaming,
"Come and get me!"

Mother of God,
she did make it to three!

OH, WE'LL TAKE HANNAH WITH US!

Everyday is an adventure
a test of you and what's new.
Since it's all new at two,
just do it and see—
eventually, society's
expectations will be
met later, alligator.

EMILY CAN COME WITH US!

"Three" must be arriving;
she's snuggling and reading,
swimming and diving,
cleaning messes and pleading
"I'm sorry I broke your doll."
Mother of God,
there is hope for us all.

WE'LL TAKE EMILY **AND** HANNAH WITH US

Was she naughty enough to be a good two,
Or just adequate?
A real handful

or an angelic armful?
You call it.
For me she was terrible at being a two.

SO HAND HER TO ME—

fun it will be
to see her through
three.

ALYSSA IS COMING WITH ME!.

Girlwind

Whirlwind visits
roil musty grandparent airs
little bodies everywhere
flying, tumbling
never walking
never mumbling

attention demanding
judication remanding

busy visits
sizzling minutes
prying digits
opening doors and drawers
necessitating tornado repair

hurricane lashings
clothes washing
bathing bodies bare
corralling, lassoing
pajama tucking
sucking cocoa straws

blizzard blows
frozen toes
red faces
hot backs by the fireplace
nearly singeing clothes and hair

meme mama,
calming marina from adventure's harms
anchored captain
steering boatlets
through life's growing storms

Baby Roomba

Room by room,
    Senja cruised—
        Baby Roomba
           dragging her broom
                In a random toddler swagger,
           engaging the world,
        acquiring her swag,
     learning from her
domestic travels.

She targeted a cabinet,
    pried open the doors
        and toppled its Tupperware
           canisters. Then turned to a drawer
                and dumped its treasures on the floor.
           Awaiting her control were
    colorful funnels, salad tongs and
grandma's tablespoon measures.

Adults in the round
    passed down
        sentence:
           Thumbs up,
               Senja, your
            performance
        definitely

    cleaned up
again today.

Fathers' Days—
Do Count

Mommy, I just woke daddy
and told him he could sleep in.

Then it dawned on dad,
celebrating father's day is,
as everyday,
about the ways and joys
of serving
her childhood.

And I have found,
grandpa multiplied,
the tables turn
and re-turn,
circles spiraling
u-turns
up and 'round.

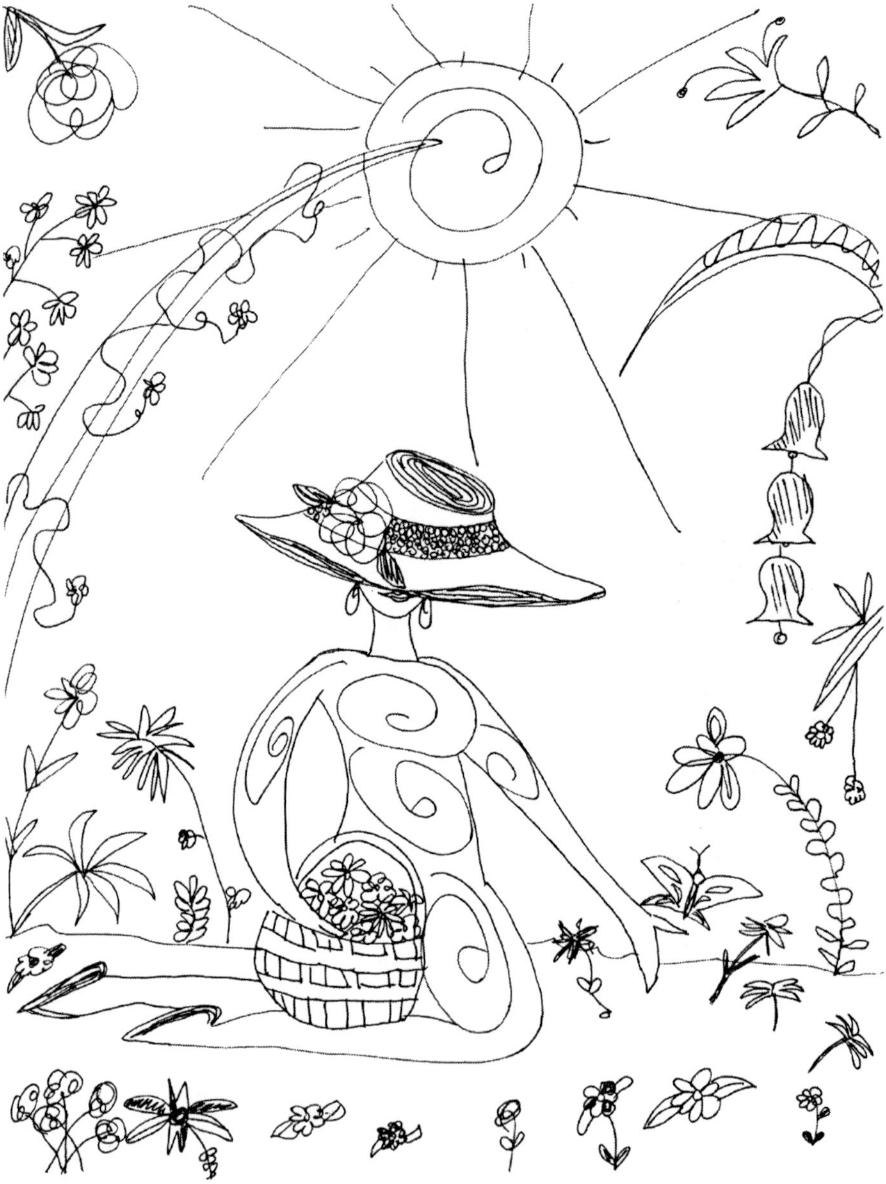

Molly in the Garden

Molly visits Florida
in the spring,
claims to visit mom and dad,
but her secret is to bring
flowers back, the ones
that wintered there,
somehow made
the snowbird trek last fall
—a mystery to all
but Molly—
she knows her plants are smart.
Winter in Michigan?
Nothing to do but lie around
and who has time for dormancy?
For once they reach Orlando
Nana and Boppa's winter warmth
bring them out to preen
and strut their stuff.
Being green keeps them from getting old
and out of shape.
And when they've had enough
Molly brings them north
back to Michigan
unable to wait to get on her knees,
dig around, weed and talk to them
in flowerese.
In record time they will stun their tans
and, if you will please, take note
of their Florida tans.

The Kitchen Truck

Alyssa and Hannah, aged three and four
traveled to a lake shore
camp ground in a "kitchen truck"
where daddy hooked up
lights, heat,
hosed in water
and hosed out muck.

The campsite was a magical place
stormy marbles rained on the roof
and acorns reigned on the floor of the woods.
Turkeys appeared with our breakfast eggs
though only the dog and Hannah saw
the "animals with only two legs."

Exploring was the thing to do—
but free of adult marinas, dams, and scenic overviews.
Collecting bugs, worms, and wood for the fires.

With many goings into the cool
and comings in to the heat
boots on, socks off
dirty feet, cold feet
became the rule.

When rain kept us trapped inside
grandma's stories brought little snugglers to her side.
Me-me, will you "make another lap"
so that I can sit there too?

What was the big hit, the favorite thing to do?
Setting our clothes on fire with campfire sticks?
Or seeing live catfish?
"Are they the fish that cats eat?"
Or was it daddy's steel-head fishing and wishing?

Probably not the place with the rocks and the dead people.
When pressed for answers the kids agreed:
Feeling the soft dead fur of a deer in the woods is hard to beat.
Adults were not needed for this,
only their ears to tell the tale to.

Uncovering the Magic

One of my fears
as a grandparent this year:
Easter's magic would fail to appear.
Were the kids too old

to drag out the stuff?
When ours stopped
it didn't get done.

WE'RE GOING TO DYE EGGS AND DECORATE CUPCAKES
THEN YOU CAN GO BACK HOME
AND HUNT FOR EASTER BASKETS.
THERE IS A NOTE FROM THE BUNNY
WITH JELLY BEANS SCATTERED AROUND.

We can make a bunny village.

IF WE HAVE TWENTY FOUR EGGS AND THERE ARE FOUR
OF YOU,
HOW MANY EGGS DO EACH OF YOU GET?

Look, they're all hide-and-go-seeking
this bunny's on guard
They want to bring the chicks to bunny town
it will be very exciting

WHERE IS THE EASTER EGG TREE?
HAS ANYONE SEEN THE EASTER EGG TREE?

I am the mayor of bunny town
and this is my crown.

They have to get all the way through bunny town to get it
and there are things that pop up out of the ground to get them.

OMIGOSH, I DIDN'T KNOW YOU COULD DO THAT

How many tablespoons of vinegar for the dye?
    How do you make turquoise?
How about dark pink?
Don't throw the dye away; I'll be right back
    I forgot to put eyes on mine
    Look, I made an Indian
I want the frog decorations; you can have the chicks

Grandma, she's taking too many!
No, we each get six! This is one of my six!

YES, YOU CAN EAT THEM
WE CAN EVEN MAKE DEVILED EGGS LATER

. . . WOW, THESE BASKETS ARE REALLY HIDDEN

I still can't find mine
I'm the last one

DO YOU WANT A HINT?
IT'S IN THIS ROOM AND IT'S NOT IN THE *MICROWAVE*
(WE HIDE IT THERE EVERY YEAR)

DO YOU WANT TO HIDE EGGS?

Yes, can we do it inside?
We did it outside yesterday

        If Jesus were an eight-year-old,
          would he celebrate this way
            with kids like ours,
    bunnies, chickens, flowers and candy?
       Maybe make up a new game?

      The worries this year were premature.
   Maybe it was Grandma Meme's fuzzy bunny ears

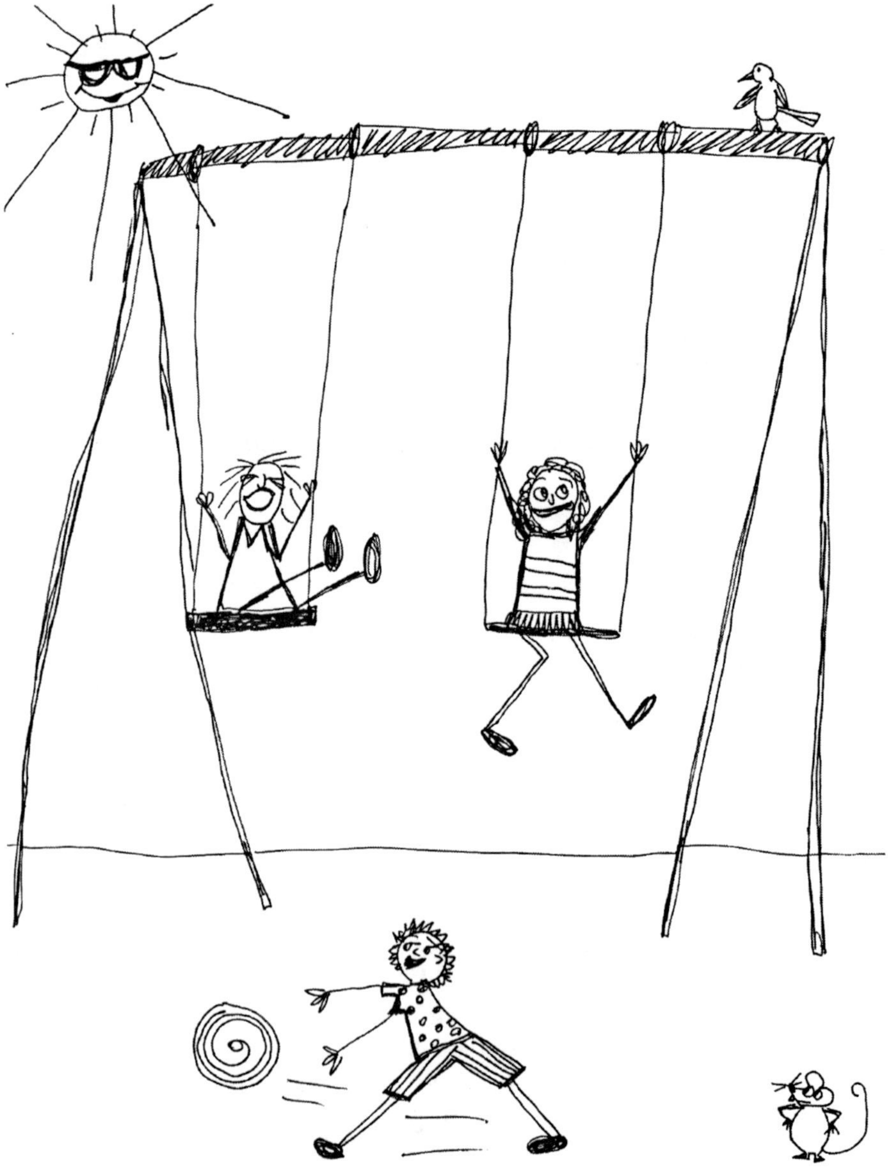

Around the Playground, Out of the Box

Parks and schools have rules, games,
and adult playground constructions
designed sans consultation with the professionals
whose job it is to use them,
that is to say, play.

Observe this one, a professional kid.
Come follow her lead if you can.
Bare your feet
prepare to feel it,
the swings, the dirt, whatever.
No matter the weather,
Shoes and socks are a bother,
If there are adults around,
they'll gather them, scattered,
so the kids can attend to what matters.

Designed as a circuit, one after the other.
Where should we start?
Swings? Slides? Monkey bars?
It seems rather arbitrary
and no big deal to me.
But to my nine-year-old Einstein
the fun was in bending the tools,
playing God with the rules,
and creating a new universe
of games and activities—
Who needs Zeus?—
and she did it in less than 6 hours, not days.

So here's what you do.
Don't approach the climber from the front
and work your way through to the back;

Climb around the outside
with your feet between the railings.
Once you have circled the perimeter
making up new challenges as you go
then approach the slide
and, maintaining the attention
of at least one adult
holler, "Look at me!"
As you go up the slide, not down
and show how the bare feet help.

Next, the swings.
Would you swing or pump?
Not these chimps.
Shinny those bare feet up the poles
and scootch across the top
Repeat as often as possible
wherever you can
anything with poles that go up
and a bar that spans

At the monkey bars swing arm to arm
then knees up and hang upside down
grab a pole and flip feet down, right side up.

Up the climbing wall in the boring way
then walk the top and jump
to the next object de play.

You get the picture—or a picture of sorts—
This report from an adult about younger sports
is clouded by the throes of culture contact distress
lacking someone to translate between groups
with uncertain overlap in languages and meanings—

all the while trying to keep track of the shoes, socks, jackets and
anything else from inside the box

Edges

Just beyond the prairie road
corn rows swallowed a town,
    whole
    towns—
        people,
who left themselves in a graveyard.
    Ancestors, concentrated in a square,
    standing out in a crowd of corn,
    conveniently located for those who care.
Nod your head as you drive by
or stop and tell the old folks "Hi."

Our families settled here—
    then frontier—
to spend lifetimes
    carving edges . . . in the ground,
Setting out
    whom they could become
    and where they could be found . . .
        safe . . .
    from the raiders
        they invaded.

There was Jeremiah's farm—
    full—
    of the grounding tools
        that plowed and raked their lives together,
        surrounding them with names . . . homes
            . . . and fences.
    Full of kids
        straining to get out
        and breathe America's chances.

Then
they buried each other.
A church yard once,
cemetery,
punctuates a sea of corn whose annual tide creep
    challenges their edges'
        integrity and symmetry.

We are halted by their sentinel:
    Plaqued words on a pedestal

        speak of a wooden church burned long ago,
            Indian wars
            and the Farrell's store.

We linger to honor those who spent a lifetime
    building lifelines to our future
by tending through their death-time
    their place between the edges,
        keeping them safe from today's invaders:
            This year, corn,
            last year, beans . . .

and by taking them with us.

For here, under our feet, only part of their journey ended.

Settlers continue their settling
    into the earth,
    our minds,
    our stories.

We travel today,
    unsettled raiders,
absconding with family stories,
    rewriting family fables,
ungrounded tools
    for carving modern edges.

Who are we?
And who were they?
What did the family do?
When?
Daddy, tell me the story again.

And the Help of Some Friends

Getting Somewhere

I am small.
Lots of places I could be,
a filler of niches
unobtrusively.

Others are tall,
shapers,
makers of niches
and the chips which fall.

Bigger spaces tempt
but mean
a stretched consequent
or two.
In the end, too many years,
and too much here
to be . . . there.

I try, from time to time,
to entice them near.
But fear their preference for
my roundness, square.

Among the Young

The young,
who won't be called old,
like to act older.

The Old
like to be thought young
but insist on acting their age.

From men in . . . hibited:
"Touch me, free me,
released
for intimacy."

And women in . . . libited:
"Release me from the feel-
-ing that touch is all there is to be."

Fears of the white—
not doing color right.

For others,
Fears started with lack of color.

Walk away
Talk away
Walkway

Look at Me

She,
strutty and bouncy
a walking teen exhibition
of torso contortions.

He,
straight, up, down, and square.
Line 'em up, line 'em up:
    Zippers, buckles and buttons.
brushes, un-musses his hair.

Me?
Number one in competitive caps.
Last year's Master's, this year's Players
Fished Michigan, marched at Selma
How about them Dawgs, and . . . Bama!

Some
like to show noshing class
with French boules, batards and baguettes,
California Napas and Oregon Williamettes.

Are you
Hybrid prissy or Caddy sassy?
Stereo rude?
Does your truck need room?

Yo,
Mama in the minivan,
chauffeur that hood.

How great are we?
Lie to me.

A Couple of Toos

I watched a man straddle a chair,
a Jimmy Hoffa henchman, maybe,
hunched at table, eyes
in a vacant stare
past her shoulder.

She, upright, hand in lap,
salad-poking busy
sprinkled the contents from
her plastic sandwich bag.

No eye contact,
as far as I could see.
No words
occurred.

I wondered about the widow by the window.
Did she want to see them talking?
And the obese man in a wheelchair
might have mused,
"They could be up and walking."

Buffet busers cleared;
others milled, refilling
water, Cokes and tea.

Gentleman Jag

travels behind
his ornament, Leaper,
and trails a quiet growl—
steward of a tradition,
the driver's car.

An improbable match—
performance car, tires and gas
with slowing owner who,
when he performed at peak
was behind a desk
or in front of a class.

But talent is not required,
maybe passion,

to share Jaguar
beauty, panache and
performance.

Can I give you a ride?
And can you abide
the scenic route
from here to there?

For what could be better, indeed,
there . . . than here . . . inside
a car that's fun to drive
at any speed?

Alas, the snag.
Jags exercise many faculties
but mine has yet to burn
any of my calories.

Junior-Senior Prom

An all you can eat parade
people and food promenade
between kitchen, table and buffet
bring your partner; choose a tray
enjoy the grand march display.

Juniors First

Culinary convenience for
super-sized bargain seekers.
lots of time in the lines,
eating done in double time
Kids beat a path
to the desserts and back

Man, wide as an aisle, side to side and front to back
Wearing jeans, boots, and a "Texas" tee, black
clears the way; his buddy: a beer gut strut.

Rumpled gent, scraggly mane
suspenders sag 'mid looping chain
unable to contain wrinkled shirt
or keep his pants from sweeping dirt.

Woman with waddled sway
Gently rocks a tee-shirted titty tent
Cantilevered over tray

Another steadies
her partner's unseen feet
plodding, in a guided stagger
O'er stomach out, head back, straight

    Their diet:
        don't get old
        lose weight one body at a time.

Seniors Last

Retirees' noon hour
running on,
seniors gather
dressed to the nines
complete with a smile
out on the town
for the day's big meal

Slimmer, survivors
jackets, vests, seasonal sweaters,
Permed hair, caps from aircraft carriers
Tech-accessorized with walkers, oxygen
and wheel chairs

They limp, lurching to the lines, hunched,
pausing, twisting, humped and caned
plenty of time for chatting games.

A curled body, hawk-nosed, caped in copper
rocking in an eagle walk, side to side,
peers down on her steam tray
prix-fixe prey

Experienced eaters
    (Soup bowls carry more dessert)
spend less time in the lines
Find their fun between tables in
Booze free schmoozing time

    "Boo."
    "Oh, you scared me to death."
    "How's our timing? Been here long?"

    "Haven't had to go see my doctor in a long time."

"I used to trade combines every year."
"What'd you get for your old one?

Especially good for the widowed male

Their diet: don't get fat; lose weight a pound at a time

Lauds

Appreciate those heroes, each
Who amaze and grace our lives
Touching us
just beyond our reach

Some can do it on the spot.
For the rest of us it takes more thought.
Jazzing their tunes,
rapping their words
rumbling and ricocheting
like trains down rails.
No planning, just doing.
We wonder how it comes about
and if it ever fails.

Others can do it anywhere.
Cameras, brushes, pencils,
easels
trace new images in empty space.
Is it magic?
What's the trick?
It almost makes me . . . sick.

Some can do it with anything:
marble, clay,
part of a tree,
shaping things
only they can see
with their special Midas vision.

My favorites build and repair
kids . . . of all ages.
Creative, patient, slow to anger.
Comforting arms, attentive ears,
and laps accustomed to children's fears
and stages.
Mapping new adventures from thin air.

Are these just skills to teach?
Or is there a special muse
infusing them,
a holy spirit anointing each
in their own productive way,
escaping the nets
of the rest of us?
Walking and chewing gum does not qualify.

T'is sufficient
for the rest of us
to make the fuss,
remembering and rehearsing those heroic tales
which define our honorific use.

Who's Your Lazarus?

A new infant
strained an old circle,
a beggar, whose benefactors gave
to let it grow.

Lazarus, I, indebted early;
now a benefactor, encounter
a Lazarus on every corner,
wanting to know
Who's MY Lazarus?

I can't go home to mother's meals.
I have to pay her due
and assisted living rent.

I can't go back to the U again;
they want to know,
Have I made my last will and . . .
Who's my Lazarus?

At the University of Lazarus
they print names ranked by contribution size,
wine and dine, name a building after you.

So we ranked ones of rank,
rank and dip our water to

our families, the needy,
and favorite diseases,
arts, culture, multiple schools
and several churches,

perpetuating old circles
with the help of . . .
taxes.

Ghosts in the Quad

We
drift in unseen
to view vacant places
when others leave.

Podiums, distinguished chairs,
or various labs—
once our commands—
now just haunts,
hallowed campus spaces

through which we used to volley
lectures, handouts,
and other old tools of the trade
at targets
claiming to seek betterment.

Now we catch our wind,
amazed at today's ways
passing through
our faded substance.

With no grindstones to nose,
nor feet to ground,
we enjoy the pleasures
of gardens, bookstores, libraries,
old pathways and cafes,
scavenging for hints of the leavings,
we once thought useful—

enough to will to a future—

which now requests
mainly money.

Over time it seems
our searches take their toll sooner.
Able to pack less,
we keep our sorties shorter,
stay away longer,
but still anticipate
the next retreat
of our campus Cancun beachers.

Your Place or Mine?

Do people perk your brew?
Motivate, energize, and keep in touch with you?
Are you on the phone, the net
Know who's where and doing what?
Good at sizing people up?
Like to meet, team, schmooz, socialize
even when relaxing?

I have friends who find that taxing.
Bad to take a rest from the rest of us,
they are on the roof shingling,
instead of at receptions mingling.
Like to get physical, morphing things with tools—
flowers on the patio
or easels in the studio.

Klutzy me, a putz with things or people.
My muses entice me inside
to dream and wander,
ponder thoughts, not groups or pots.

What excites or comforts you?

Do you dabble between talents,
change leopard spots?
Your genius may be . . . balance.

Wherever you like to hang your hat
may you visit it often—
and get away from where you're paid
to race those rats.

Beauty Pallor

Ole' to the senoritas
fighting the bull
from an endless cue
of toros.

Horns lowered,
eyes glowering,
staring
at a Mexican market stage,
we stood,
    separated from—
    yet red-cape-tivated by—
the beauty of
a Mexican songstress
reigning
    with a Latina flair
from her mariachi band—
    firmly in command of
        the music—
        and us men
        standing
in a crowded market square.

Petite, stately,
with long black hair
    ribboned at the waist;
dark eyes emanating grace—

A visual feast:

To us, inedible,
with a taste:
    At best, imaginable

and only from afar.

Car Wars

It was a topless day in the summer in the city,
sun raining shine on the streets.
Cars were out because they were pretty
not because they didn't leak.

In the sun on the street
sat two old buddies
in an army Jeep,
three restored warriors
from a pre-Hummer era.

Two seasoned sports in their summer shorts,
    sitting with a slouch on the seats of a Jeep
tanned legs, sandaled feet,
matching
    white socks with hair
        and
    hats with posture.

Their Jeep, topless,
    olive drab paint
from a long ago war
    white stars and an army logo
narrow knobby tires
spare on the back
    perched proudly
cruising quietly
    ferried the merry military vets
    into a world war skirmish
        with Jags and Corvettes,
        Nissans and Mercedes.

The trio advanced
> one stop light at a time,

winning one more war,
> hearts and minds.

We Experience our Backyard

Dinner With Theater on the Lawn

One of the bunnies was munching the yard
nibbling, nosing, twitching the air,
senses attuned to the dog straining hard
to breech the porch and chase
its movable feast.

There were birds nearby, safe on their feeders,
seed eaters enjoying dinner with theater.

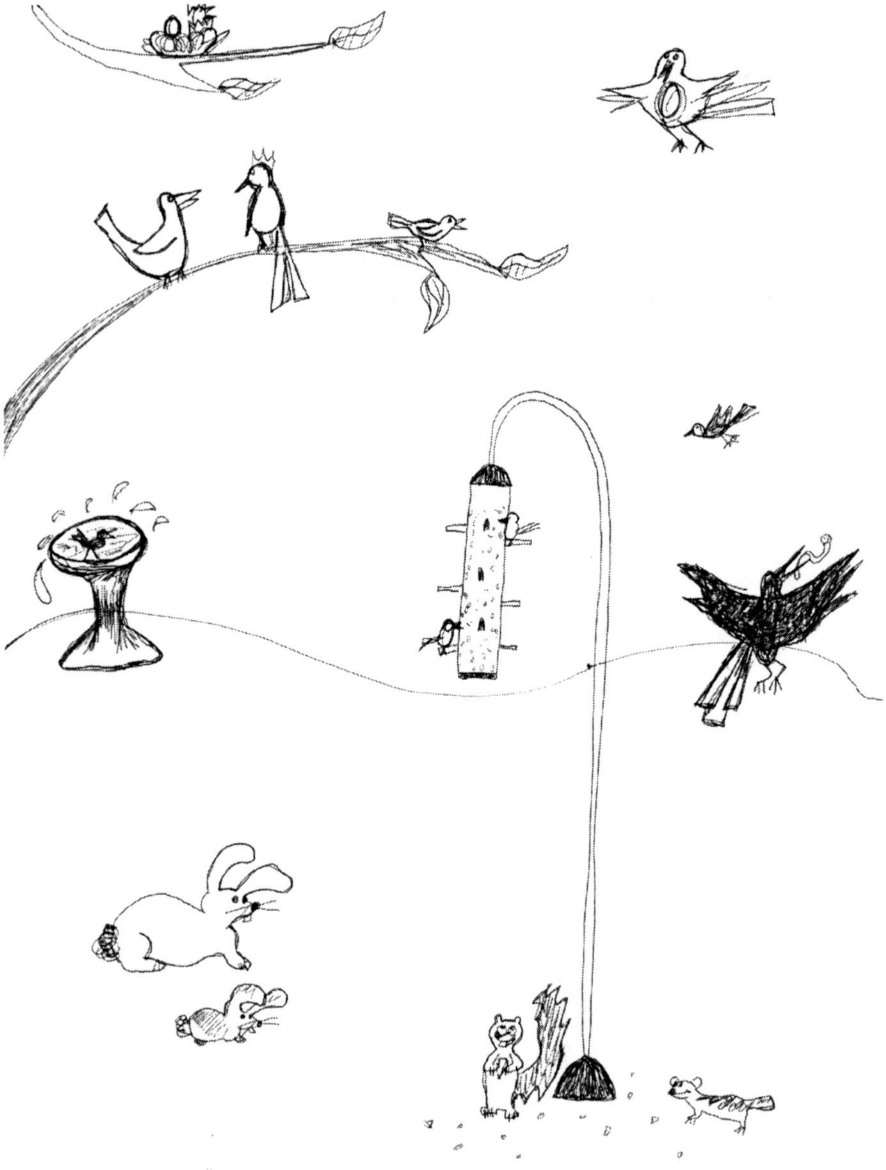

The Last Bird Words

The roll was taken from the porch,
    in whispers,
of those who came to our backyard church
    for vespers.

Neighborhood redbirds
and red breasts arrived
with the slipping evening light
to claim their first-come, first-served
roosting rights.

Their evening duel ensued
o'er who would have
the last bird words.
The redbirds, last at the feeder,
    chirped it shut for the night,
but couldn't out-wait

the robins'
slow, drawn out antiphons,
    warbling down from the trees,
    trailing silence through the leaves.

These psalm-like prayers
prompted amens
from those below
not too busy to care
    who sang when
        or if the last solar lantern
            came on before ten.

Backyard Summer Drama

The last dog walked
and garage rolled shut,
backyard stirrings cue
the porch's invitation
promising tonight's
summer evening presentation.

Take a chair
dim the lights.
the curtain rises . . .
to heavy muggy air
settling, darkening to night—
harkening the first fireflies . . .
Stage left, then right.
Rise and disappear.

Cricket interludes intrude—
scattered . . .
building . . .
pulsing . . .
to a surround sound
insect etude.

Rock it, cricket, rock it, cricket
rock it, rock it, rock it, rock it, . . . ,

From a tree,
Excited chirping
sears the air—
trumpeting tension.
Unseen.
Where?

Minute gnats
take the air bringing

twisting bats weaving
through their dinner space.

Then long-awaited fireworks
slo-mo, everywhere
rise and disappear—
a firefly ground finale,
ballet sans choreography
the heated evening mating urge, severe.

Rock it, cricket, rock it, rock it, rock it

A stir of breeze;
showers rattle the maple leaves.
The drama cools.
Night's curtain falls.
Time to exit
reluctantly

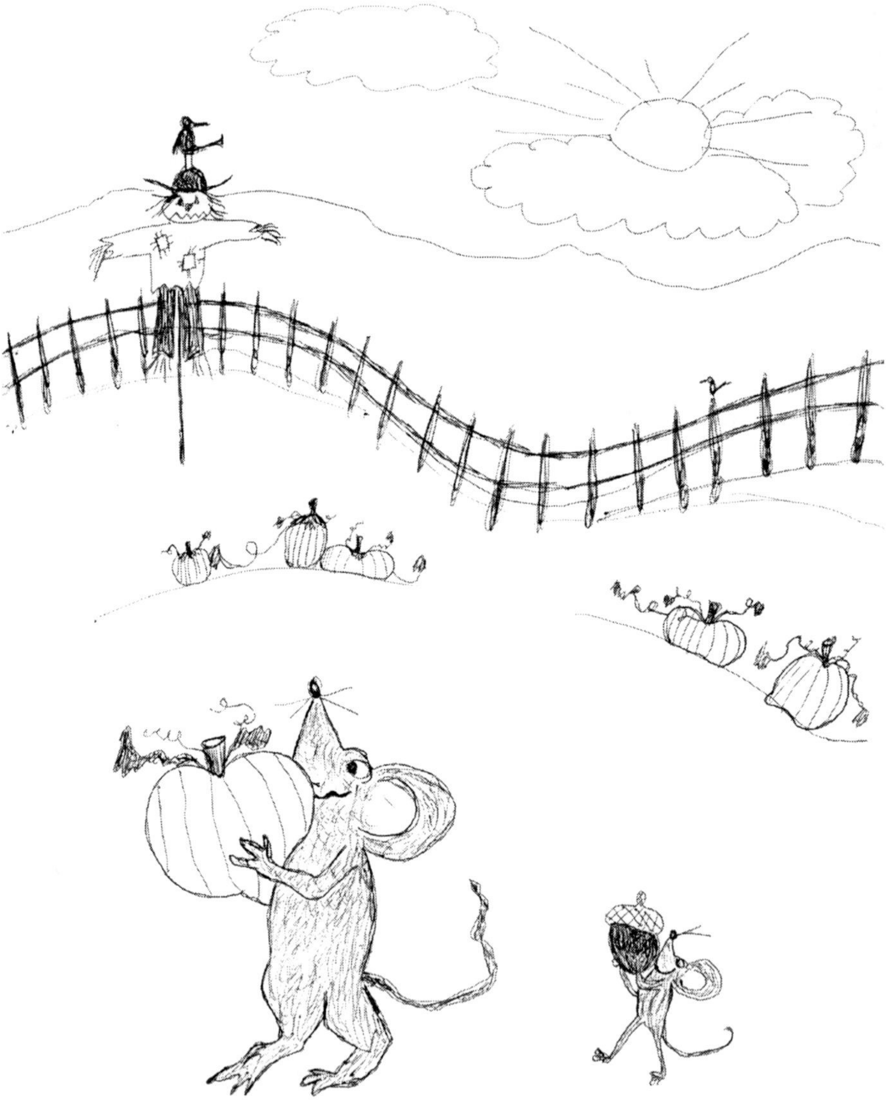

November Between

Spring drama and summer booty, now cached,
once again Mother Nature changes hats.
Gaudy October has yielded
to muted November's aging fields.
The many shades of brown and gray
underscore the shortening days.

At the fence, long rows
of brown corn stubble lead
to a spray of empty trees.
    Fans framing space
with limbs,
once lost in summer's earnest greenery,
now, chilled,
reveal the interstitial beauty
of their gray twigged filigree.

Come inside.
Let's toast nature's annual evening time;
    Let fall your leaves,
      and sag your sap.
Enjoy Mother Nature's windy music in the cracks.
We'll light her logs and pour her wine.
Anticipate.
    She'll soon unpack

        her stunning winter wardrobe wrap.

The Hawk Feeder

Morning glides by,
sipping coffee
at the bay
window,
looking through

to a nervous world
of bird squalls
twitching
between
bush and feeder.

Squabble, jockey,
grab and go,
shelter,
food,
can't chat

always
eyes wide
elsewhere.

Blurred shadow,
empty silence,
huddled safety
of a tangled vine.

Inside, away from
the backyard pandemonium,
pinch a few flakes for Charlie, circling
his aquarium.

Backyard Hummer

Hover in the air
on your way down there.
Dine at the window;
perch or whirr.
Four parts water,
one part sugar.

Dennis R. Keefe

Other Special Places

A Beach Night Plug

Lines of lanterns weave
tropical paths,
    manicured
    as only Florida condos can,
and beckon me
on the balcony
looking down

at footbridge shadows
    framing air;
arches
lifting away
from the day
toward waves,
sounding in the dark.

Flood-lighted
palm fronds
undulating in the breeze
teasing me—
exercising octopi,
    knees up, on their backs
    playing keep-away
    with a beach ball,

while
through the door . . . left ajar
Reality TV intrudes

Descend? Leave the other three?
Rude? Or
opportunities to explore
for poetry?

Hiking Yellowstone

A guided group hiked a mountain wood
        Most to learn;
    One for solitude.

We were told the hikes would be flat.
We were not told: compared to climbing ladders.
We followed our guide,
Up the continental divide,
    where east-flowing rivers went north
    and west-flowing rivers went south,
And down
    through competitive strata of spruce and lodgepole pines,
    Darwinian winners in the ecology of fire.

She shared her expertise
and ecological lore
about calderas, buffalo wallows
and other ecological havens
as well as osprey aeries—
or were they only ravens?
About heat stressed fish
and creel kill,
the sixth kingdom, Archaea,
pictographs and fire strikes,
obsidian, travertine, rhyolite
    and sinter.
Signs insisted:

    DO NOT ENTER

Fumaroles, geysers, pools and mud pots
    steamed,
warming and warning
those who stopped

STAY ON THE WALKWAY

From time to time a stray went ahead
or lagged behind
to admire a bed
of Fringed Gentian
then bend low
to photograph western mistletoe—

> less intent on learning about mountains
> as from them.

Wordless lessons from nature's many podiums
stirred newly alerted imaginations.

> Of swaying pines, where dancing coniferous boughs
> and sunlight whirled
> introducing the loner
> to a brave old world,
> > whose persistent sharing
> > prompted, here and there,
> > unsettled stirrings about caring.

> And of whispering creeks pointing up hill
> to waterfall photo ops,
> a natural gift to be shared by all.
> Is there a place to send a thank you card
> or do we let the subject drop?

The stray was each of us
in our own due time,
sensing the surrounding wisdom
> there before the time we came
> and long past when our children come.

Huron Shoreline

Welcome to the waterfront
neither sandy, preened nor beachy keen;
only the hardy need apply
for this Upper Peninsula hospitality.

A rocks nest monster
bone yard of
craggy stones strewn
to wrench sandaled feet
and keep us at bay,
away from Huron summer play.

A promised roast daunted
by gulls taunting the children there
tossing marshmallows
out to share.

Returning, we
watched our steps
to miss
the grass geese messed
and guessed with guarded thanks
the best was yet ahead.

Dead End

The Mission Peninsula road would end, said the sign.
But a circle sent it back where it came.
Opposing scenes,
Different lane.

It will end in rubble,
Advancing stubble and weeds
But not as long
As it meets our needs.

The Point of the Mission:
Oral Emissions
From Mission Point

Where once it was deep
the lake now reveals
its rocks and sandy spots.

Was the water too low or the land too high?

If you asked the bay, it receded
and invited the beach out to play.

The peninsula argued
it stuck out its tongue to extend the beach
and spat the rocks into the bay.

The lighthouse, unbiased,
from advantaged stand,
probably knows, but is closed
and has nothing enlightened to say

Either way,
tourists were challenged to come and play.

Cameras clicked and children balked
While park hikers walked
and a daddy and daughter waded, feet wet, in water.

Bird watchers followed a spit
out fifteen minutes before getting wet, their
binoculars arcing the horizon wide
or swaying on necks
with cameras, side to side

Two bike guys paused.
"So far, so good," was heard.
Then off, a few yards down the road,
to stop again at a cherry stand.
Waving vendors, girls, the likely cause.

Peninsula pit-spitter professors met nearby
      (In Traverse City it's cherries)
to advance their techniques and see
how far their pithy products would carry.

Whether lob or dart,
high tech or low,
phloop or fart,
wi-fi or blow,
they focused their eyes and marked their pits;
fellows would follow for pith and a prize.

Lighting a Mall Pall

Antlered,
belled, trimmed in red
—oversized poster glam
in a men's wear store—
a lifeless image
modeling holiday hospitality
fostered, for those on the move,
the illusion
of cheer.

Seated at a cafe',
I returned the stare
inert.

A woman stooped to greet a child
then eagerly await
news of his day.
Her focused smile,
filtered through tangled hair,
decorated my holiday.

Fire in the Peat!

Wet-kneed cypress sloughs
home to swampers, 'gators, and peat:
The Okefenokee,
quintessential swamp,
Now a tinder box—
Waycross, Georgia,
at the mercy,
of lightning strikes and lighted butts.

In this corner
Unseen fires,
scattered and counting,
spread smoke fog
among the pines—long leaf,
loblolly and slash,
tall, stately, tilting
at the encroaching
shroud.
Slowed traffic;
an acrid campfire ambience breeze creeping
to Jacksonville today
and Atlanta tomorrow.

Yonder,
command posts batch and sort
mixed rigs—
    Firefighting's this and that:
    pumpers and pickups
    every known shovel and axe.
    Trucked Cats, inching to the staging areas
        four-hundred-fifty-dollar-an-hour dozers arched
        blades down on flat beds
    await

California Shoshones
the Wyoming and Minnesota Big Rock Units,
Texans and the Carolina DNR—
    Firefighters sporting badges and tees,
starting the day
at Shoney's Breakfast Buffet.

    Refrigerator art on the walls—
    reviews from grateful schools—

    rave:
        "Our heroes are firefighters"
        "We love our firemans"
        "Our house"
    saved.

At the bell
crews rise
head rigs to the trees
go toe to toe with the smoke and heat.
They, need no sleep,
are easily flared by the smallest breeze . . .

Day's end—no worse.
The heroes' hope,
some calamitous douse
to restore the swamp and send them out.

Can you bring yourself to pray
for a hurricane?

A Rube Cubed

Sense and the City

Amazing doers use
talents, wit, their ability
to make sense of a city.
With the energy of youth, they
are eager to pay
two cents dues
for what's to take
and make of the city's vibrant synergy.

We who care
about the fare
enough to pay for what they do
rely on those with a nose
for where the action is
And so the city goes.

Cents and the City

The city sent us—
hoofers—noting:
Where's the beef?
The high cost of space, we mused
left no range for rovers super-sized.
Walk them about,
stack them up,
and so the city culls.

Individuals come, aiming high, bound
to make some noise
but somewhere along the rise
to the tops of the rocks
the sounds puree
and so the city mulls.

For my money, a prairie guy,
accustomed to horizontal
not vertical
don't come here with vertigo.

Scents and the City

In the city we went looking
afoot among the 'hoods
poking noses into stores
seeking special foods.

We elbowed our way
through Zabar's nasal overkill
of tilapia and basil,
shelves of teas and bries
walls of tins, toffees,
open barrels of coffee beans
Ethiopian, Jamaican
Yirgacheffe blue mountain style,
smells of whitefish, lox
salmon and trout mixed
with tuna,
seeded, filled, dilled or sesame'd.

Down aisles where cases displayed
bleu cheeses, rude
bakery aromas intruded
on olives, pickles, and other
potent pleasers.

Outside,
vendors competed through open doors—
cupcake stores,
chocolate delis, luncheonettes and diners,
all hawking scents in the city.

And so the city blends.
Osterized olfactories send
from many aromas, one
morphing city scents companion.

For my two city cents worth,
I, the prairie guy,
lilies freshen a mixed bouquet
but we struggle to note their
special flower way.

Chaos in the House

Waitress flicking water;
wets his face.
A tease? A test?
A glare.
Mouthed threat.

They don't stress the service here.

Regulars coffee-tarry
in a harried atmosphere.
Smothered and covered by
dawdling waitresses
ignoring those at the door
eyeing space progress—slowed—

no Houston in control.

Cook's excitement at the grill
a lightning spin, cop a feel
tickle a waitress

behind.

At the counter,
order-bacon in the air:
customer's loss, floor's gain.

didn't see a thing.

Dirty dishes piling
under the collective nose
waiting for to go.
Empty washer closed.
Blame's the game;

So are argue and ignore

Piece-meal:
"Your bacon's on the grill."
Meanwhile,

grits and waffle chill

Dare try
Look 'em in the eye?
You order straight ahead;
they hear side to side—
Behind-the-counter politics;

Leave YOUR stories at the door.

Tink, tink.
Thought I ordered water.
—in a glass—

Thanks, I think.

Sign Irony

The sign on the Rhinelander
cemetery road seemed clear:

NO OUTLET.

But I wondered,
who reads signs
on the way to six feet under?
Or who needs a sign to remind—
isn't "plan to stay" implied?

Maybe this graveyard's ground
poses special risks
above and beyond
our common lot,
recycling an earthen mix.

Could the sign reflect
a local spiritual nihilist's wish
to discourage the passage
to an after-life?

Or maybe it's some Wisconsin existentialist's
take on Sartre's "No Exit?"
Locked in, sure, but,
with whom . . . or what?

Then I thought of the signs on café doors
that welcome customers with OPEN,
then when it's time to go
declare the outside CLOSED.

Had I thought to check this road sign's backside, might
I have found, "Y'ALL COME?"
Redundant? Or just truth in advertising?

I decided it wouldn't hurt to become more wary
of the rules governing my cemetery.

A Vineyard Picnic Space

A summer breeze stirred the boughs
of a Douglas fir
and scented the shade settling from above
while from our feet,
    cascading down,
a hillside of grape vines
advertised
years of cultivated love.

Crosswinds of charcoal-seared aromas
      teased noses
          with picnic promises,
while the circling host and hostess
    decanted vineyard hospitality.

The day's camaraderie, once stirred,
seemed to parade
lingering first at the baby's crib
then, circling, radiated outward
to the perimeter.

At moon-rise
    solar lamps directed
the darkening, angled
    walk back
    down
between tangled
    vines and lives.

Thanks to the Gladharts

Maybe Next Year

Pot holes occur.
But work on the roads?
Maybe next year.
Hope does endure—
see the suggestions below—
for those who drive
with the discipline required
to avoid the distractions
driving pleasures and civilities provide.

"Think less about driving fun,"
would be a good Rule One.
Focus on the surface,
not the scenery
or driving leisurely.
If you must have fun
leave your car behind
and take a 5- or a 10-k run.

A mechanic replaced my car's front spring,
realigned the front end,
charged me five hundred bucks,
then recommended
"Drive slow," Rule Two.
Won't please followers
of slow-driver me.
But the goal of pot hole
management is
not their happiness.
Traffic is a distraction to ignore.
Watch the road, not someone else's car.

To see pot holes coming
use Rule Three, namely:
"Don't follow closely."

We prairie guys value elbow room,
but here they treat space as a liability.
Pass, change lanes and cut to fill in.
Time to make space a friend again.
Defend it against the cutters-in.
The discipline is—
if it's traffic, ignore.
The communiques, the body language
of drivers you can't satisfy—
let them rage.
Avoid that hole!

Yes, "Avoid those roads full of holes:" Rule Four.
Follow the roads still drive-able—
out of the way, to be sure
but detours capable
of protecting your car
while getting you . . .
who knows where.
Unfortunately for me
that's my whole neighborhood.
We have invested so much in schools
we can't afford the roads
to reach them.
Could mean home schooling for the grandchildren
but I can't be sure.
Unable to get out there since the January thaw.
Now it's April and our hole bumper crop has really matured.
I'll see the kids again,
but in the meantime I continue
to search and share word
of roads that are good.
If you live at the end of one of the others,
maybe next year.

Ain't We Got fun

In The Mornin'

Newspapers, bagged and looped
o'er my '47 Schwinn,
pedaling east on a paper route
I encountered a mountainside
bordering my Minnesota prairie town.
The sun, about to crest, would
light this ersatz phenomenon,
expose its prairie absurdity
and shoo it off with the morning dew.
I had to hurry to cruise its
short-lived vistas
and exotic avenues.

In The Evenin'

Seated, wearied, in a western hotel bar,
we watched a Wasatch evening Alpenglow.
Sunlight crept up the mountainside
as the evening lifted the day away.
A sequence of hillside nighttime lights ensued,
featuring a red
flashing "U," which . . . they said
meant the Utes
had won another game.
Celebrating, we ordered another round, the same.

In the Meantime, In Between Time

From a low swale of creek-cooled air,
and damp-enhanced aromas
of magnolia, pine and pulp mill sulphur,
a wrist twist sent my Honda responding.

Its twin cylinder cycle vibes
thrust me up the far side
of the road dividing Georgia's red clay earth
into the evening's displaced warmth.

Ain't We Got Fun.

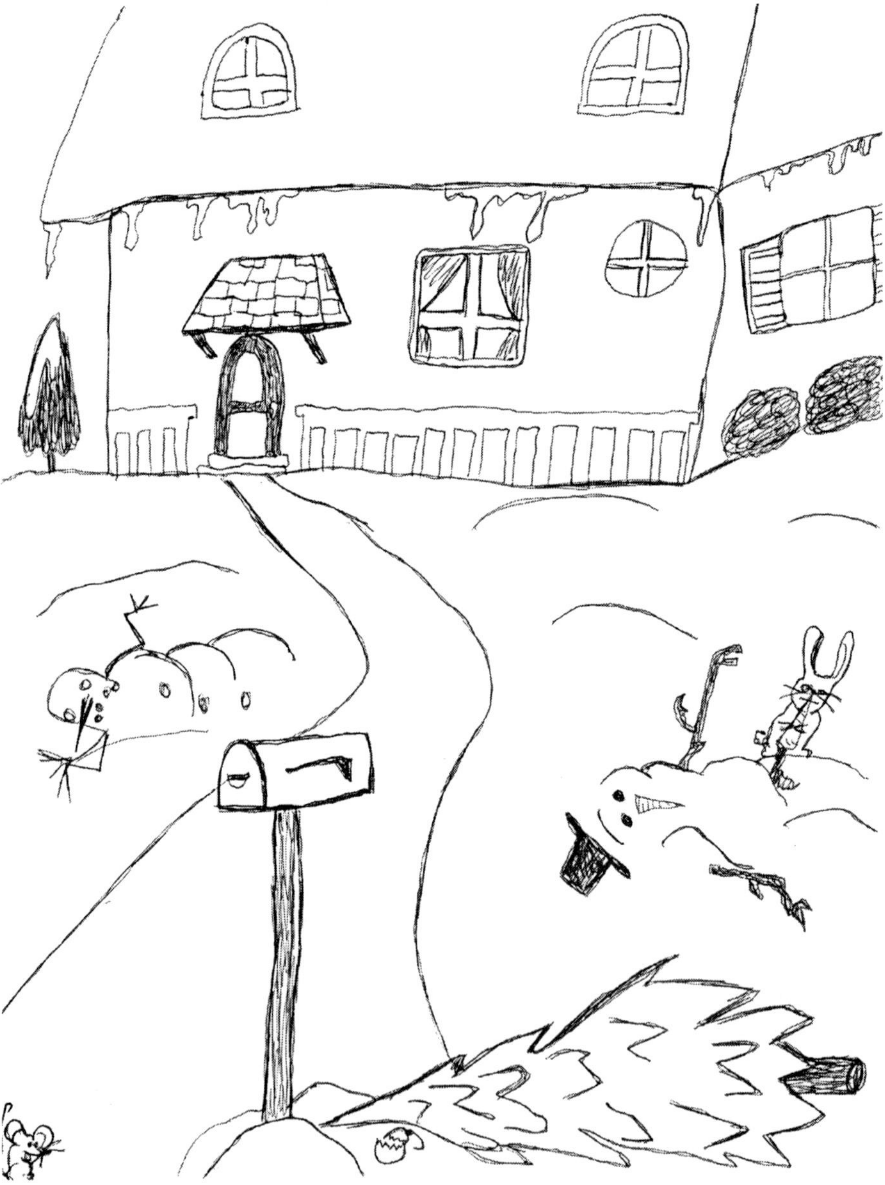

Holiday Travels

We primped and prepped
for holiday events
that came,
rocked and rolled for awhile,
then passed so fast—
      to the last tree needle swept—
I decided to examine where they went.

The white Christmas which arrived on cue
took five when warm winds and rains
sent snowmen, in a panic, running
to
      the
           city's
                drains,
their graveyard of arm litter

          u
sticking   p

in the little snow that remained.

Our out-of-town revelers traveled
once the holidays died—
back home, the phone verified.
Their colds, flu and holiday blues
had hitch-hiked to meet new friends.

Holiday foods, once so special,
are now huddled in the cold,
their trip to the trash or disposal
left over for a couple of days or so.

And those festive decorations, wrappings and bows?
In the basement, stowed.

Others, led to the curb, await years
of breaking down barriers
with new landfill neighbors.
In the midst of it all we were treated to a
warm weather . . . backyard . . . raccoon . . . winter . . . resurrection

                surprise

which entertained us two days.
Fur, focused, rooting in birdseed spilled
eventually disappeared under the deck
and left us to wonder . . .
Are we included in their plans for
longer term tenure?

The tree, we undressed,
then let free, yes, free to be
a green recyclee.

But there the trails . . . begin . . . . to . . . . fade.

Interpretations made
about Christmas,
hidden in memories diverse,
left when our visitors dispersed.

And, somewhere, misplaced,
is my taste for
outrageous
holiday decor.

The News From the Cruise

BEGAN

on a Tuesday
Not this or last
but in the past,
with rumors from the net
about excursions, arrangements
packing and documents

AND WILL END

on Wednesday,
not this or next
but when memory wanes
or someone says,
"Please, there's no need
to tell it again."

PREPARE

to wear . . .
what . . . on the sea to Alaska—
to experience . . .
what . . . places exotica,
people reachable only by air or by sea?
Will it be sunny all night,
full of cold ice?
They can leave you at the dock, it was hinted,
if you misread a form
or left it at home not printed.

GETTING THERE

In Flint,
a lady with a laptop
couldn't keep her trap shut
talking at a business man
sitting on her left

switching to a cell phone
in her right
when it wasn't typing
tippy, tap, tippy, tippy, tippy, tap,

Atlanta displayed
between Concourses A and T
life size airport art from Zimbabwe
Sculptures done
in Spring and Serpentine
stone

Young man, plaid shirt,
earnest attempt at a beard.
He, attached to a cowboy hat
not nearly as attached to him.
Naked nervous moments,
de-cap-itated,
when he stumbled through
the cramped doors
of the airplane loo.

First Sightings

On the left, looking up,
the mass of Mt. Rainier displayed
while across the aisle, we looked down
at the rest of the Cascades.

Kids limo'd, rock star style
long, black car, to Seattle
"No pictures, thank you!"

SEATTLE

Cascades to the East
Olympics to the West
Docks to the world,
Ferries to the burbs.

The inspiration
to a coffee boom somehow
missed our hotel room.

Rode the elevated to the Needle,
Monorail Ale,
and looked down at a map.
No, wait, that IS Seattle.

Lovely parks downtown
home to those without—injured,
now insulted, by those who seek attention,
the costumed and painted
young, on parade.

Down at the lounge—
like the hotel, big city small—
I settled for a few
minutes to check for news from the muse.
Bar tender busying, table to table.
Hotel patrons on elevator detail
pulling luggage over tile,
clackety click, clickety clack.
No use.
An evening martini . . .
not up to the task.

Pike's Place Market

Acres vending everything fresh
Watch the seafood fish throw show.
Especially fresh today,
tee shirts to go.
SHIRTS FOR PERVERTS
"It's not pretty being easy!"
Two for ten.
We escaped and lunched
Bolivian.

TO THE SHIP

Tetris driver stacked
luggage, us ten—ovation
in his taxi-van.

EMBARKING

A smooth sail through
document checks,
those things you do
to get people and stuff
on a ship for a cruise.
Anxieties allayed with each gangplank stride,
able to focus on why we were here,
the excitement of what we would find inside.

A week's worth of clothes
soon disposed to the drawers
and corners of efficiency quarters.
Time to take command—
captains of our staterooms—
on the Westerdam.

ON THE SHIP

one of those dam ships
from Holland America Line

Our Stateroom

Efficient space—for all
but elbows,
on main deck, above steerage
and the Irish
rumored below.

PROMENADE:

MIND YOUR HEAD
WATCH YOUR STEP

Take a walk
three decks up,
outside.

Pools

A retractable lid for the kids' rock and roll pool
that swayed with the sea
more than nine decks below—
a slow sideways list, or,
when the sea was heavy,
sloshy-wavy aft to fore.

Adults in posh hot tub thrones
watching the kids encourage the slosh
—were seen less often, swim clad,
in the brisk Alaskan air of their outdoor pool,
except for the day
they swam in Glacier Bay.

THREE LAPS TO A MILE

Doesn't that couple know . . .

DECK RUN IN PROGRESS

. . . that's the wrong way to go?

Blasts from the horn in the fog

I hope,
out there in the mist,
you're not near
enough to hear
this.

LOWERING STATION
KEEP CLEAR
LOW LIFE-BOAT CLEARANCE
ASSEMBLY STATION

Ours is thirteen—
women and children in front—
respond when they call your name.

Dining options

Formal, casual
sit down, buffet
a grill by the pool,
service in the room,
coffee shops, lounges
and snacks in the bars.
Soda cards on lanyards—
their many punches
survived a week of kids' snacks,
dinners and lunches.
Friday's late night highlight,
a chocolate extravaganza
photo op
and finger food frenzy.

Buffet

Asian,
Mexican,
On and on,
Italian, Deli,
Bistro, Desserts,
drinks and pastries,
all known food groups, and
a new one invented just for today.

Dining Room

We sat and "selected'
from a menu
—not "Either-Or," but "Why Not More?"
every dessert, multiple appetizers, and a couple of soups.
Then tried all entrees not seen before
and maybe not again.
With Dutch coffee, Java smooth,
we ended, Indonesian.
The multi-menu'd kids
tried Alaskan king crab and gazpacho
with their fries and cheeseburgers.
On formal nights we dressed better
but maintained our old eating behavior.
On the day of the baked Alaska bakers parade
we saluted the chefs
and the culinary magic they made.

Crows's Nest

Glass enclosed
full frontal viewing area.
Pilot your own ship and check
the library's coffee shop—
to your left
or the lounge and piano bar on the right.
Journaled from 10 decks over
the Pacific O—
Seattle to Juneau
and back.

DESIGNATED AREA FOR PANAMA CANAL PILOTS

Why not?
A ship with a life!

Ship Mates

The young or beautiful, it seems,
cruise other seas or other times.
We did wear beautiful clothes—
maybe not beautifully
but with effect.
Logo'd tees advertised
our clan, the race we were running on deck
or where we were from
—and, of course—
our sizes.
Even our canes, walkers and wheelchairs
we sported with pizzazz.

BLANKETS FOR DECK CHAIRS

employ a man
to bring them out
and put them back.

Shopping

Learn to vacation the American way.
Our seminars prepare
smart shoppers for duty free sales
and Alaskan gem shopping excursions.
Let us teach you about tanzanite
expose you to topaz
or upgrade your diamond
then unveil Alaskan jade
at our Northern Lights Collection.

If you're game, take the lessons
on how to use our casino
or enjoy champagne, get in on the action
while learning the art of collecting
art;
then join our end of cruise auction.

If you're going ashore take our seminar for
how to shop in port.
Get coupons and precious gem
certificates the shops will mount for a fee.
For the kids, free
furry pins or
plastic rings—they change colors.

You will find
available everywhere
grizzly paw salad tongs
Ulu knives, fleece,
smoked salmon
and furs.

HELP US KEEP THE OCEAN CLEAN
DO NOT THROW THINGS OVERBOARD

The wake frames
low sun over high mountains.

Everywhere on your promenade,

viewing snow capped mountains
and listening to others' conversations.

ASEA

Daytime temp, 50 degrees
10:20 sunset
four o'clock sunrise.

GLACIER BAY

First Sightings

Water spray,
small wisps, spout.
Milling fins stir
water textures.
A fin, a fluke, out,
down and away.
With luck, pods.

Bears, only two seen

Brown, hard to see,
yellow, browsing,
over the hill,
gone.

Black, moving
along the shore
among the greens.

Ice chunks

float past,
increase,
hitch-hiked by puppy seals,
sense water is better
and slip over the side;
details missed by seagulls
but not by two berg-surfing eagles.

Glaciers

16 at tidewater
100 alpine
The Great Pacific, covered in black, receded
too balanced to move.
We watched Margarie,
groan and crack its way
between mountains
five feet a day
then send blue chunks splashing,

with mini sonic booms,
into the bay.

How well equipped are you
to wait
and watch plate tectonics
move?

Juneau

Behind the docks, mountain walls,
narrow Juneau,
no roads in or out.
They shovel snow, inches
measured in hundreds
courtesy
of the Japanese current sea.

Couponed shoppers, their first opportune,
rush to mine gold
bargains at Juneau's jewelers,
see the capital sights
and the Red Dog Saloon.

We headed to the woods to a musher camp
eager for immersion in the lore
of sled dog breeds,
their care and developmental needs,
the time it takes to build a team
and more.

We knew the original Iditarod story
and Balto's glory
but not Togo's work
or what it takes to qualify,
winning sprint and mid-length races
as well as the sponsors needed to pay
to race today.

A sled dog ride, six to a cart,
gee-hawing through hemlock trails
led by Iditarod mushers
who signed our caps
then taught us to socialize dogs
—by letting us pet their pups.

Sitka

Good news, folks,
the lifeboats worked,
tendering us in to the world's largest city—
thousands of square miles,
a volcano, mild climate,
Russian souvenirs and legacy.
A walk in the park with totem poles led
to a place doing raptor repair,
a small Russian church—
walls of icons, a sailcloth ceiling
and red Bishop's chair.

The kids wondered if the eagle on the cross
was a bird of pray.

Ketchikans

complain about the rain and collect
totem poles, eagles
tourists, summer merchants
and salmon in fishing boats with nets,
We learned, touring on a duck,
quack, quack, quack
between a bunch of corny jokes
QUACK, QUACK, QUACK
that they live—on docks—
a lifestyle blasted from rocks
and meet their exercise needs
by climbing steep wooden "streets."

Victoria

Most went to see Canada's jeweled
city of castles
with flowers in parks and hanging in baskets
while I stayed
to watch a mock
pirate battle regatta
in the bay.

And Some Amazing Events

An M & M Wedding Toast

We have witnessed
Myque and Marya
publicly commit,
and "tie the legal knot."

And I am here,
a little nervous
and a lot proud
to toast that knot
aloud

but also, as a dad, to note
that the knot . . .
. . . while legal, . . .
. . . simple
    it's not . . .

Come, for a moment—below the surface,
where poets sometimes lurk
and see the complexities of marital reality
Myque and Marya have stirred and stoked.

Senja,

has expressed *this* concern:

MOM, DAD!!!

Was our old way so bad?

I was learning new tricks
and saw you both gloat.
Will this wedding thing
rock our family boat?

Aaron and Molly, Kelsey and Louisa

This wedding affects you too.
The bar has been raised; expectations renewed
you can search for awhile
Google mates by the mile
but eventually,
    well,
        you get the idea.

One last complication.
Myque and Marya have forced the hands
of two widespread clans
into a kinship alliance
that goes against tradition.

Yes, By linking estates in Ann Arbor and East Lansing
they risk our long standing traditions
of biased loyalties
and competition.

Just ask any of the family delegates
How many days and nights of negotiation it took
to get from "Go Green!" and "Go Blue"
to "Peace, man," and "We love you, too."

Because of these "clan-plexities"
negotiators from **the Keefe and Peters families**
do extend their apologies
for the length of time it took
to hammer out this merger
make it legal
and get it into the book.

But we finally made it—
Myque and Marya persisted
insisting it could be done.

We have a new game here,
where love wins—
something really important, for a change,
that we can *all* cheer.

So, let's celebrate **Myque and Marya**,

and the many *gifts* they have bestowed
to enrich our lives:

> Senja, of course, but also
> love and family commitment
> new friends and kin folk
> theater and music
> even the go green/go blue peace

The list is just beginning to grow.

Friends, will you join me in this toast:

Let it resound:

May peace, prosperity and happiness abound!
May they flow through today
and into the future
to increase
every time Myque and Marya turn around!

CHEERS!!

M & M: We love you.

Thank you.

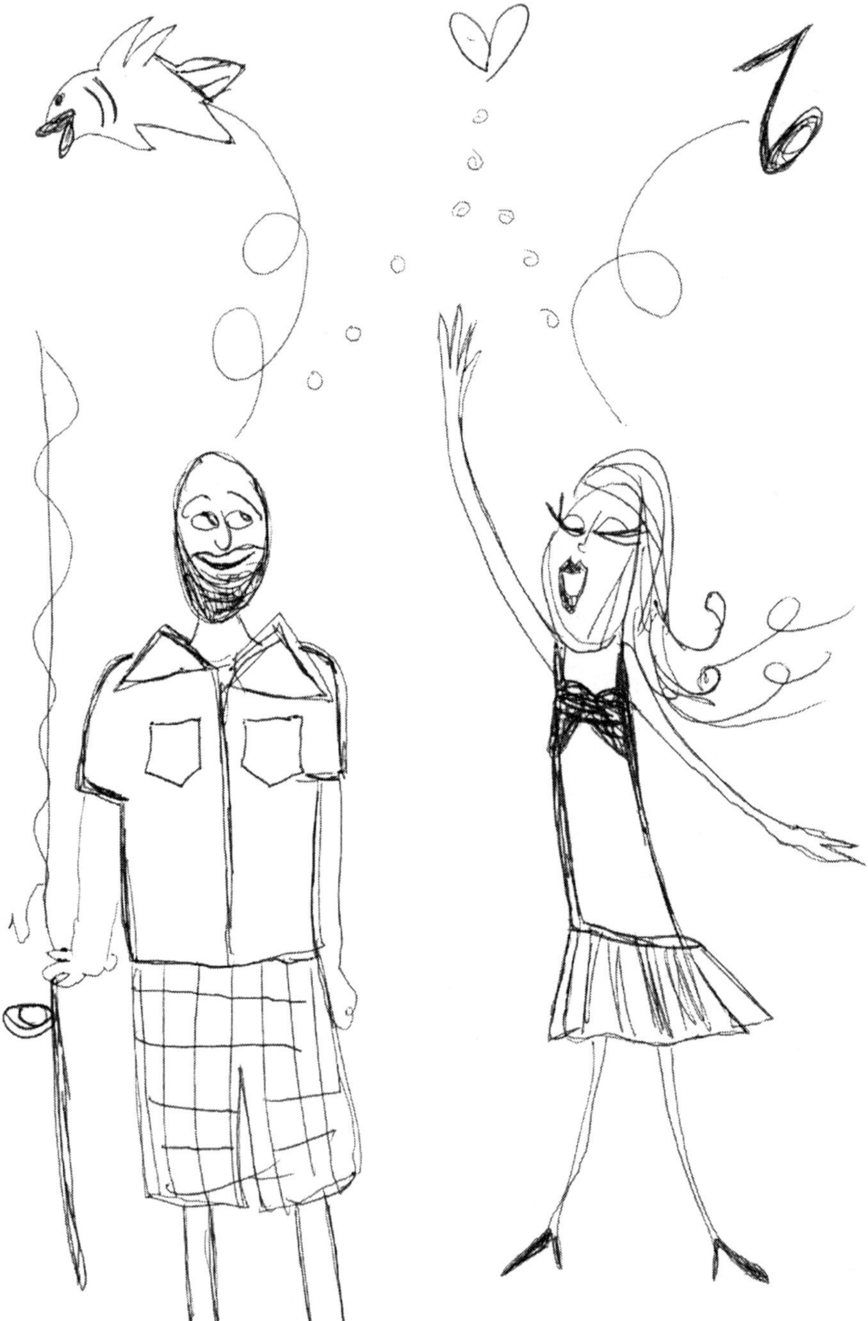

Nouveau

"Do whatever He tells you."
Words directed at Molly?
Quaint words out of place at a modern wedding?
.... The words are not new.
At a wedding in Cana
     2,000 years ago
a compassionate guest spoke those words
     to an empty-handed wine steward.
"Do whatever my Son tells you."
     The steward listened
          and was rewarded
               Water was transformed into wine
               a wedding celebration was preserved
            And an embarrassed host was let off the hook.
And thanks to that attentive steward, we were ALL rewarded
          with a WEDDING STORY—
          —   of Jesus' first miracle.
That story in John's Gospel
has allowed Mary's wedding exhortation
to continue down through the years
     to modern brides
     their grooms
     and, indeed, to all of us:

"Do whatever He tells you."
Mary's son is still speaking.
Is anyone listening?
Could we, like that ancient steward,
cooperate with God
in the transformation
     not of water into wine
     but of old lives into new loves?

Molly and Aaron listened . . .
Were they rewarded?
    . . . with MIRACLES?
   And a new life?
You make the call.

Does it sound probable to you—that
MOLLY, . . . ,
   unquestionably unique
     professional musician
     world traveler

SHOULD FIND AARON . . . ?
   just as unique
     registered nurse
     outdoor enthusiast?
Somehow, these two unlikely partners were prepared—for years—
   for each other . . .
and brought together in our midst.

A wedding miracle?
To me, a miracle of discovery!
It began in a Montessori School
and a hospital emergency room.
Ask them to tell you the STORY OF THAT "MIRACLE."
Like many good stories, It will have an effect on you
it made me WONDER.

Here's another miracle story.
It's about SHARING COMMITMENT
Aaron and Molly,
   unlike SO many others,
    have found their pearl
      the one to sacrifice all else for
    that special couple's world
      between individuals
      that rubs them together

>   warming them to commitment.
Hang around them for awhile.
Get them to talk about the commitments they are making
to people and ideas
>   Some close to home,
>   but some far beyond . . . themselves.
Like many good stories, we can see ourselves in them.
I have seen the consequences of their commitments
to me and those close to me
and it makes me THANKFUL.

Any story of their wedding
will have to include the MIRACLE OF CREATION—
Something from nothing!
>   A new blend of families and careers
>   house and garden . . . made over
>   new traditions building . . . one day at a time
Get them talking about their plans and the work they have already done.
Like a lot of good stories, this one will ENERGIZE YOU.

And, finally, staring us in the face,
>   indeed, bowling us over,
is the ongoing saga—we all love to talk about—
of those daily, miraculous awakenings
>   To . . . What their children are teaching us
>   Olivia, Alyssa, Hannah, and Emily
>   Pulling us out of our meager selves
>   One hug at a time,
>   One profound question at a time,
>   As only children can
>   Toward . . .
>   The DISCOVERY of love
>   As only children can
>   The COMMITMENT to its call
>   As only children can
>   And our personal dance with CREATIVITY

>   Especially around our homes and families.

Remember the love stories involving these children
If you're having trouble DISCOVERING LOVE,
these will help you.

Yes, there is still some wine left in that ancient Canaanite tale.
Like good wine John's story has aged well.

> The flavors, aromas, colors and after-tastes—of that ancient story
> are still blessing us . . . with weddings
> and their miracles today,
>> —new vibrant life from where we let it go stale.

Such love stories, in the hands of good stewards
can mature and sweeten
> from vintage *wedding* stories
> to *marriage*, ... *family* . . . . and *"beyond"* stories.

We all have our own love stories.
Let's steward them well.
> Retell them,
>> regale others with them
> but above all,
> listen to them,
> and listen IN them
> for Mary's Son

And dwell on whatever it is He may be trying to tell us.
It will be about love.
Can we say we prayed?
> Will you witnessing here today say . . . "Amen?"
>> "So be it!."

Credits:

The words, "Do Whatever He Tells You," and a mosaic of the wedding scene in Cana can be seen in the chapel of the parish church of St. Thomas Aquinas in East Lansing, Michigan.

"Water Into Wine." Sermon, Rev. Karen E. Gale, Edgewood United Church of Christ, January 14, 2007.

Gospel of John 2:1-11

Travels to the Sun

A Midwestern ode to those Metros who slog
south . . . to find the sun
wasting distemper shots on their dogs;
and
to those special few whose homespun grace
helped us learn
that Spring is more than a sunny place.

Expectations were high!
    It was March . . . and Spring was due
        . . . on the calendar.
    de jure,
    If NOT de facto

We decided to act . . . to
    . . . Tampa with the temps,
    hit the trail, and travel back to
        a Florida place . . . called Saddle Ranch.

We traveled south,
    left the FRIENDLY Midwest,
        drove through southern HOSPITALITY . . .
    . . . and seemed to overshoot our mark.

For, while the weather said, "Tropical,"
    we met some kiesters,
    chill-winded Nor'easters,
        who blew in with a cloud
        covered Spring with a pall,
            and fostered ill-will . . .
            . . . and loud noises.

For suddenly sun had sounds:
    Horn blasts . . .
Making beach life feel like home,

home on the RANGE,
      home on the FIRING range . . .
           of a city intersection.

Want to get picked off in the cross-fire
      of honking horns and honked off drivers?
Ease away from a stop light.

It got worse.

Horns, not deadly or personal, enough
     Were focused . . . by loud
people . . . creating a din
     spewed from urban
         lives spent wrestling crowds,
           where rowdies
             have their way every day.

   "You idiot! Can't you read the signs?"
   "F—you, genius!"
   "I'll Call the cops!"
   Enter more horns—cum blasto!

No wonder the crowds spit them out
     and sent them south,
         bumper to bumper
         blasting away
         shooting lip from the hip
           mile after mile
           wild west style . . .

        . . . until they settled
          into their old ruts,
             repeating the retorts
               transplanted,
          where sand dragged them to a stop in the sun,
             adding outside burns
               to their inside ovens,
          extending to others
             their hellish hot city covens.

It's possible that this was all too much
for a first time snowbird
       unseasoned, senses askew,
              over-hyped illusions
unable to generate enough internal personal spring
to tune out the cacophony.

There may have been poetry in the voices there
Some were trying to communicate,
but they were strangers
and they seemed insistent
on trying to communicate via their cars

       we seem capable of merging lanes,
but not people
       traveling enclosed
              in dueling vehicles.

No wonder roads rage.

We did finally hit our mark,
       our Mark and Tracy Spring,
              complete with alligator . . . and darts.

       Host and hostess
       with the "sodas"—
              not the "pop"—
       drinks and paella all around—
              it never stopped.
Was it warm?
       on the porch
       by the pool
              anywhere we were.
And were we cool?
       all, way cool,
              especially when the cameras came out.

There was Hannah
      with or without a banana;
Emily and Alyssa never missed a
      cheesecake opportunity.
Uncles, aunts, moms and dads,
grandmothers and papa
friends, dogs,
Brie's monologs.

We finally located spring
 . . . in the midst of what we were doing.

Olivia Turns Seven

Olivia is getting old, she
used to be just three, four and five
yesterday, six
I'm told she'll
next be eight,
and eventually,
eleventy-eleven.
But today it's the switch
to SEVEN and . . .
. . . time to celebrate!
The presents await—
but, first—
let's "CUT OFF THE CAKE!!" *

* an official Olivia-ism

Are You Being Served?

Need some time off with TLC?
Visit the Chaska Millers,
Midwest's friendliest Grill
and B & B . . .

Also, . . . , occasional aviary.

For things to do
check with Barb, the concierge.

The menu, extensive;
the service will bring
you back again.

But don't leave until Gary has washed your car.
Or
ask to park
in their garage.

Give Me a Break!

Brendan's coming home, I heard,
vacation visit
from the desert,
    one of those places
    with the warm oases.
Has he been given the word
about the hard
winter we've had,
to be prepared
for what might be incurred
while here?

Officers are used to
being served.
Time for him to recall
Ordinary Guy again,
to deal, for awhile,
with the issues
we combat day to day
fighting for peace in the U. S. A.

Last week, typical
Thursday, a rough day
at the coffee shop,
war zone tough.
The customers, a noisy bunch,
and I don't mean musical,
made it hard to read or write
    —pity those holding their breath
    for theory and poetry—
or a quiet lunch.

Nor do I like those wooden chairs
on which we sit in our ca-rears
    the risks we take
        in necessary sedentary tasks.
            taking on the weight
            of the world.
Somebody needs to, it seems
and, disciplined, we obey.

I take mine with sugar and cream.

And at the end of the day again
into the couch I eased
while Carole mixed the gin
martinis.

The rest of the week, about the same.
Long Friday lines at Kroger's cashiers,
waited for a lap pool lane Wednesday
Sunday's sermon ran overtime.
    —Not good pacing for Brendan on vacation—
But waiting's not my game.
Get things over faster, I say.
Why can't we just get in, do it, and get out?

Nice to have "mess" ready with the Mrs.

This was the weekend the students chose
to fling, their annual spring . . . riot,
a rite
of passage.
But do wonder—
Someone needs to recruit that energy,
to blow things up

where the local businesses
don't complain so much
about collateral damage.

Thank heavens for those evening neck massages.

Monday and Tuesday, baby sat
Kids, cute,
stress.
Like an Iraqi soldier
not well trained
for policing chaos.
I am bailed out by Carole.

Bottom line,
we've no military codes,
no George in charge.
I fear Brendan may feel at odds
wandering,
at large,
wishing someone would
keep us in line.

How long must he
experience this disorder?
Talk to Karen.
Build a green zone.
Keep him in
away from the cold,
protected,
warm.

Go for it, Karen.
But bring your "A game".

Movers and Shapers

God breathed,
inhaling to her bosom
lovers, seekers and God wrestlers alike
to refresh us
in the breath of
our collective air.

Long charged as life shapers,
and sent forth a career ago
to baptize professions, families and
others who happened along,
now brought together
to gather,

with Christ in the Guter's backyard

for a reunion,
unlike others—no casuals assembled
but those who had tilled
in the gardens of
each other's lives,
putting up memories along the way,
now to be opened, celebrated
and assessed

as life on the verge

threatens to travel
further towards away
or at least merge
to another lane.

We acknowledged, losses:

Most notably, the marriages,
cymbal clashes
to our vulnerability.

Then the
missing pounds
scattered around
several
making the group look better
    If that were possible!

        But mostly we dwelled
           on the gains:

Those careers, last seen
beginning to bloom,
now, fading, trailing
achievements and seeds
for our succeeders.

Children, trajectories repeated,
extended our families
and initiated our after-lives.

A new spouse pictured
with her wedding band
waits to share our love first hand.

Old angers, faded,
newly piqued today
by current perceived dangers.

The new gray hairs and wrinkles,
neither overlooked
nor overdone,
tradeoffs for a lifetime of wisdom,
hard won.

Our love, circulating,
the tip of a berg,
substantial, hidden,
nudging others
in a persistent drift
toward its fluid, endless end.
The biggest gain?
Our stories, approaching lore.
Unable to remember fast enough
we laughed, searched for more
and chalked each one up
as the world shaking event it por-
trayed. What, indeed,
was the "Golden Guter?"

                Then God exhaled

a Pillars'
senior diaspora
to seek late-life vineyards,
seasoned vines
tangled and tired by the hurly burly

with the challenge·

            RESURRECTION

God, bless our tennis!

Be a companion
to those with whom we taste our wine.
Hike, T-bar and ski with us.
Be the muse to
our writing, painting, singing and gardening,

the thorn to pique our questions.
Disturb our comfort,
goad us on,
no time for death,

                    as we anticipate
                    future breaths.

A Pillar Raised

It was mid-summer, the end
of a mild July,
when the news arrived—
summer shattering, life-staggering—
the sudden loss of our "Pillar" friend,
Mary Ann.

It was her last summer
that brought together
the rest of the Pillars.
There was nothing we could give
but share the grief and the news,
incomprehensible,
of futile tries,
and compare
under a steeple on the hill
what fraction of her spirit
we could muster
to get us as gracefully through.

But there we were—
watching her come back home—
Burlington on the river, Iowa.

It was the 22nd of July,
Mary Ann's last full day.
The Church feted another Mary
from a village on the water,
Mary of Magdala.
She, too, had gone seeking the Lord
through the darkness of a tomb,
persevering while others came and went.

The first to see Him, risen,
John said—sent

to spread Easter's words.
"I have seen the Lord."

It was the end of summer
that raised concerns—
going on without the warmth.
For Mary Ann took the secrets
that warmed the lives
of Mike, Mary Jess,
and a list
too long to count.

Mike's loss,
his lover, the only one
who knew his past.
Mary Jess,
her future, mother-orphaned,
no mom to be aware.
And on down a long, long line.

For us, she,
always ready to talk,
left, unable to say goodbye,
but now transformed: our first
to see the risen Christ.

The rest of us, aware of the line
in which we stand, ponder anew our chances to join
the struggles, the joys and everyday noise
of sharing His news,
the meaning, unique
to each of us.

Pillars, rejoice for a life well done
and let us all say, "Amen!"

Two Queens

Gargoyles perched
on Mary's church;
buttresses flew
o'er fenestration blue.
Chartres' ancient hands extend
to yet one more pilgrim band.

Saints, sinners, citizens,
common and royal—
statues, weather-grained,
usher visitors through portals
to darkened
mystery spaces, designed
by masons.
Crusader booty from Arabia,
they crafted pointed arches and porticoes
with compasses and
arcane mathematical ratios.

The gray ghost-lit columns
prop pointed arches—
and greet,
guild by guild,
    window by dedicated window,
the furriers, the tanners
the carpenters, and coopers,
the stone workers, the shoemakers
glass makers and bakers:
    first come, first served builders
still attending Mary's sacred maternal court.

We approached the crossing
with measured steps:
nave, apse, choir, transepts.
Honoring Mary at center court.

Mother of Him,
mediator for all who seek,
patient moderator of their childlike rivalries
(Rose colored political volleys
launch across her throne.).
Her grand vista: round windows,
roses,
ancient glass
passing left, right and center,
jewel-lighting her sacred space.

Back home,
in a white lighted,
     medic space, mystery free,
a town lined up to see
a dying country queen.

Unaware of her care-giver court,
and white curtain vistas:
     children, friends, waiting,
     assisting,
     time running short.
No eternal favors to give,
her family not divine,
she still united her pilgrims one last time—
a collected expression
of today's goodby,
missing mysteries of the yesterdays,
that fed her generation
and led them to their time to die.

Events
would send her
through parlor, church, procession and tent.
We came to honor and remember
an old life newly spent.

Atop the earthy end
of what remained

roses' pained aromas
were left to ascend.

our star shooting through the night

in that lovely dwelling place

trailing their effects
through town

Outside in the night

Lighting Veterans' Day

Our oldest light,
long in dim,
leaped,
recharged,

    Our star shooting through the night,

on veterans' day

    to a site
    unknowable
    but boldly measured.

"Woke up this mornin' with my Lord
Hang on, Jesus"

—her Lord of the living and now the dead—

"Woke up this mornin' with my Lord . . ."

. . . in that lovely dwelling place

where the Sun,
withholding no favors
bestows honor
on mothers
and others
who walked uprightly.

Another light to magnify the Lord.
Another light illuminating ancient words
to bookmark our lives.

Inside, we greet,
view what's left

and ponder the rest.

Outside, in the night,
parade lights form,
and stretch the street
back up the hill—
glowing lights
blinking, milling,
building
momentum—

some running mini laps
around girl scouts' caps

then,
illuminating our holiday choices,

move away

    trailing
        their
            effects
                through
                    town.